The Peter Paul and Mary Song Book

Photographs by Barry Feinstein

PEPAMAR MUSIC CORP.

NEW YORK, N.Y.

Peter

Conflict has shaped my life. I approached my classmates with the same openness and trust that I had experienced at home, but few of them spoke the same language. In P.S. No. 6 (at 85th and Madison in Manhattan) status was achieved through possessions. I tried to obtain recognition by excelling in the classroom, then I worked hard in the after-school hours trying to convince myself and my friends that I was really a very clever fellow who was putting on a big act in school just to fool the teachers. My life changed abruptly when I was graduated from grammar school. I was permitted the luxury of having four years during which everything I valued was similarly valued by everyone around me. The High School of Music and Art was an adolescent's Shangri-La, a unique wedding of social, academic and creative lives. All the art students (I was one) played the guitar and knew songs of freedom and hope. Often, in the last hours of a party, we would weep together in our awakening to the knowledge of a man's love for his brother. In the fall of 1955 I entered Cornell University. The very first day I began to wage a terrible battle inside myself. The campus was magnificent and the course both difficult and exhilarating, but the students themselves challenged the way of life I had learned to love. The fraternity system ruled, and the social mores were completely alien to me. I tried to conform. I joined a fraternity and, to tell the truth, I loved the people in it, but I could never get used to seeing the "rushees'" hurt faces when they were rejected. In my senior year I became aware of the historic import as well as the emotional power of folk music. I was president of the folksong club and produced Cornell's first series of folk concerts. When I was graduated in September, 1959, I intended to enter a school of design a year later and, in the interim, to try to earn money by singing. My first engagement was at an Israeli coffee house in New York. Once a week I played for $15.00 and all the food I could eat. A month later Eliezer Adoram asked me to join the Aviv Theater of Dance and Song, for which he was musical director. The members of the Aviv imbued in me an exacting standard of performance. They taught me to respect the profession I was becoming a part of. I decided to work alone, and my break came when I was asked to perform on the television spectacular, "Folk Sound U.S.A." in June, 1960. Albert Grossman introduced me to Mary, who had already been singing with Paul. Gradually we all began to believe we might have something to say together. It appears that I have partly resolved that conflict of which I spoke. I am glad these conflicts exist, for without the ability to sense the world around me, without the desire to evaluate it for myself, and without the capacity for caring about what I see, I would never be able to sing folk songs.

My Dad says that once, when I was very young, we were driving in his old Chevie convertible and singing "The Too Fat Polka." We were both singing the melody, and then he began to harmonize. He says that I stood up in the front seat and laughed so hard I couldn't sing anymore. I'd never heard harmony before. I guess all that happiness in my ears was just too much for me. That was when we were still living in Dorsey, Maryland, where I was born. Because of my father's work we travelled a lot in the car and the three of us used to sing to pass the time. I think the first time I knew I could be something more than a casual entertainer was when I was called back from my freshman year at Michigan State to do an assembly for my high school in Birmingham, Mich. I'd worked before, but that was the first show I'd ever carried by myself. At Michigan State University I played and sang my own songs and country music, and I emceed *everything!* I was even elected the third ugliest man on campus in my junior year. I got a job in a camera shop in Bryn Mawr, Pennsylvania, and began saving money to go to New York. I won an advertising contest for a series called "Man With a Camera." The prize was $467 worth of flash bulbs. I turned them in to the store for $60 which brought my savings to a grand total of $500, and I was off. After three weeks I was down to $26. I was on my way home when I stopped in an office that manufactured and developed photographic chemicals. I asked for a job as a salesman, was hired, and in less than a year, was production manager. During that year, I went down to the Village to a place called The Commons and played chess after work on Tuesdays. Then one night there was a stage in place of the chess boards. I asked the new manager if he was looking for entertainers. He said sure, come try out. I did, and began to play there regularly. Pretty soon I was dragging in to the office late all the time. I knew I had to decide which it was going to be. I decided to entertain. At The Commons, I did songs and emceed and did sound effect imitations. It was there that I met Mary, the freshest, most beautiful thing that had ever walked through that door. Soon after that I moved to the Gaslight where we began to do guest sets together. Then Peter met Mary, Mary introduced me to Peter, and soon the three of us started to work up numbers. I knew Al Grossman, but I couldn't imagine that all this was leading some place. Peter was the one responsible for getting things going. I just didn't believe what was happening. Now I take care of the books, financial wizard that I am. Musically, Peter and I have versatility and quite a range, but what really makes us different as a group is Mary. I think she's the one who has a future in show business, perhaps as an actress as well. I'm not ashamed to say that my goal is to save the world. True communication of thought and emotion for all men! Music is a way of achieving it.

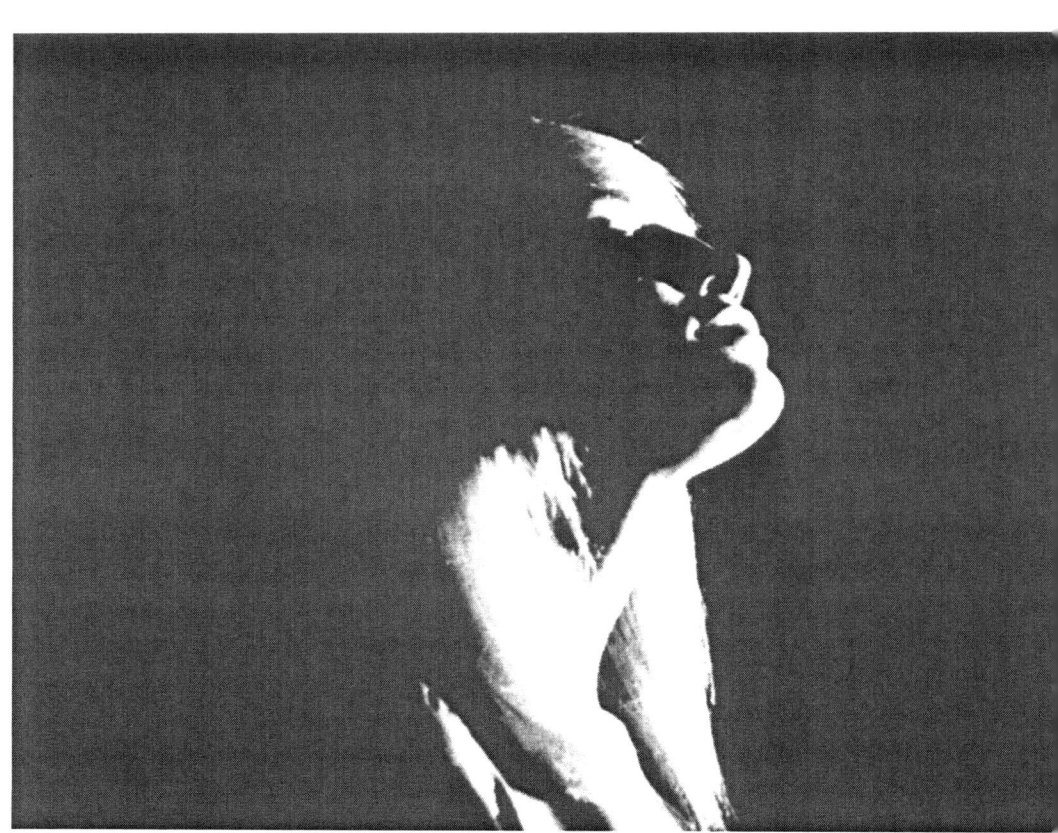

I could tell you in words that I was born in Louisville, Kentucky and that I was raised in Greenwich Village and that I had a lonely childhood and that I love nature, but when I finished telling you all this I don't know whether I would have communicated anything at all. Yet, in folk music I find a way of saying everything I want to say. In the audience response I feel other people saying, "Yes, I understand," "Yes, I feel that too." "Yes, that's what I want." I feel a sense of continuity with history and with the folk music that reflects it. I like to think when I am singing some of the early American folk songs that members of my family sang these songs when they and the events that evoked them were new. I come from a long line of non-conformists. My mother and father are both writers and were always united in presenting to me a rugged distrust of "the establishment." I was surrounded by people who did things or were trying to do things . . . artists, writers, people who were intense about life and who wanted to affect the world they lived in. Like most young people I rebelled, but even in my rebellion I never got very far away from these values and attitudes. I did not make the voyage through adolescence easily. Unable to be like everybody else, I was equally unable to be myself. I didn't know who that self was. I'm still learning. I never planned to be a performer. Still, folk music was very much a part of my life at home. Like many other young people in Greenwich Village, I gravitated toward the Washington Square Park folk-sings and the neighborhood coffee shops featuring equal parts folk music, chess and the talking artists. Although everyone I knew was busy doing something or getting ready to do something, it never occurred to me that I might ever "do anything" with music. What artistic drives I may have had found their expression in reading other people's words, looking at other people's paintings and moving furniture about to make the two rooms in the apartment do the work of three. Then I met Paul, and we did occasional guest sets together at the Gaslight. Al Grossman introduced me to Peter, and I introduced him to Paul. Soon the three of us were working up numbers together. When Al took us under his generous wing, I suppose he and Peter and Paul expected something to come of it all. I didn't. I think I really went along for the friendship, the sense of belonging. I can't write about Peter and Paul and what Al has done for me—for us—without an intensity of feeling that stops the words before they come. They have given me myself. They are, for me, what all the music is about; integrity and love and the reality of feeling. If this vision that we share with you in our music has proved to be successful, it is not, I believe, because it is our vision, but because it has been yours all along.

ARTIST REFLECTIONS
- Peter Yarrow 5
- Paul Stookey 7
- Mary Travers 9

SONGS
- ALL MY TRIALS 90
- A'SOALIN' 50
- AUTUMN TO MAY 20
- BAMBOO 38
- BIG BOAT 86
- BLOWIN' IN THE WIND 44
- BLUE 104
- COME AND GO WITH ME 130
- CRUEL WAR, THE 28
- CUCKOO, THE 124
- DON'T THINK TWICE, IT'S ALL RIGHT 46
- EARLY IN THE MORNING 12
- FLORA 68
- FOR LOVIN' ME 134
- GILGARRA MOUNTAIN 119

GONE THE RAINBOW	17
HUSH-A-BYE	71
IF I HAD MY WAY	23
IT'S RAINING	32
JESUS MET THE WOMEN	116
JIMMY WHALEN	122
MAN OF CONSTANT SORROW	30
MONDAY MORNING	126
MORNING TRAIN	54
MOTHERLESS CHILD	128
OH, ROCK MY SOUL	99
OLD GOAT	58
ONE KIND FAVOR	108
POLLY VON	79
PRETTY MARY	62
PUFF (The Magic Dragon)	41
QUIT YOUR LOW DOWN WAYS	96
ROCKY ROAD	74
SINGLE GIRL	110
TELL IT ON THE MOUNTAIN	82
THERE IS A SHIP	114
THIS TRAIN	14
THREE RAVENS	112
TIMES THEY ARE A-CHANGIN', THE	102
TINY SPARROW	65
VERY LAST DAY	94
WHEN THE SHIP COMES IN	136
RECORDING INFORMATION	139
INDEX OR FIRST LINES	140
CHORD DIABRAMS	
Ukulele	142
Baritone Ukulele	142
Tenor Banjo	143
Five-String Banjo	143

This Train

WORDS AND MUSIC BY PAUL STOOKEY AND PETER YARROW

© 1962 PEPAMAR MUSIC CORP. (Renewed)
All Rights Reserved

16

Gone the Rainbow

WORDS AND MUSIC BY PETER YARROW, PAUL STOOKEY, MILTON OKUN & MARY TRAVERS

Autumn to May

WORDS AND MUSIC BY PAUL STOOKEY AND PETER YARROW

© 1962 PEPAMAR MUSIC CORP. (Renewed)
All Rights Reserved

If I Had My Way
BY REV. GARY DAVIS

© 1962 PEPAMAR MUSIC CORP. (Renewed)
All Rights Reserved

Man of Constant Sorrow

WORDS AND MUSIC BY PAUL STOOKEY AND PETER YARROW

© 1962 PEPAMAR MUSIC CORP. (Renewed)
All Rights Reserved

It's Raining

WORDS AND MUSIC BY PAUL STOOKEY, PETER YARROW AND LEN CHANDLER

© 1962 PEPAMAR MUSIC CORP. (Renewed)
All Rights Reserved

Bamboo

BY DAVE VAN RONK

© 1962 PEPAMAR MUSIC CORP. (Renewed)
All Rights Reserved

Don't Think Twice, It's All Right

BY BOB DYLAN

Morning Train

ADAPTED AND ARRANGED BY ELENA MEZZETTI

© 1963 PEPAMAR MUSIC CORP. (Renewed)
All Rights Reserved

Hush-A-Bye

ADAPTED AND ARRANGED BY PETER YARROW AND PAUL STOOKEY

© 1963, 1964 PEPAMAR MUSIC CORP.
Copyrights Renewed
All Rights Reserved

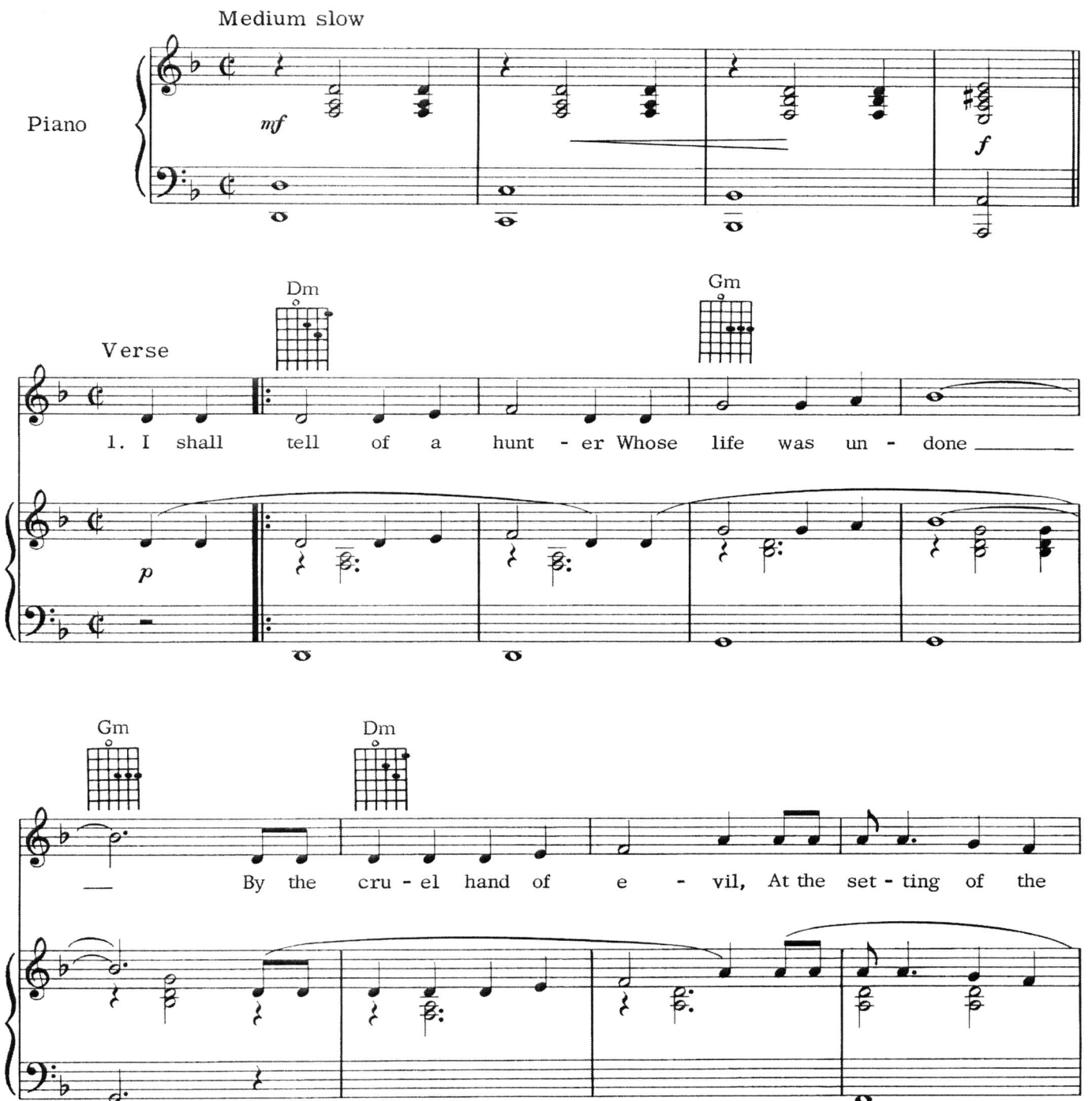

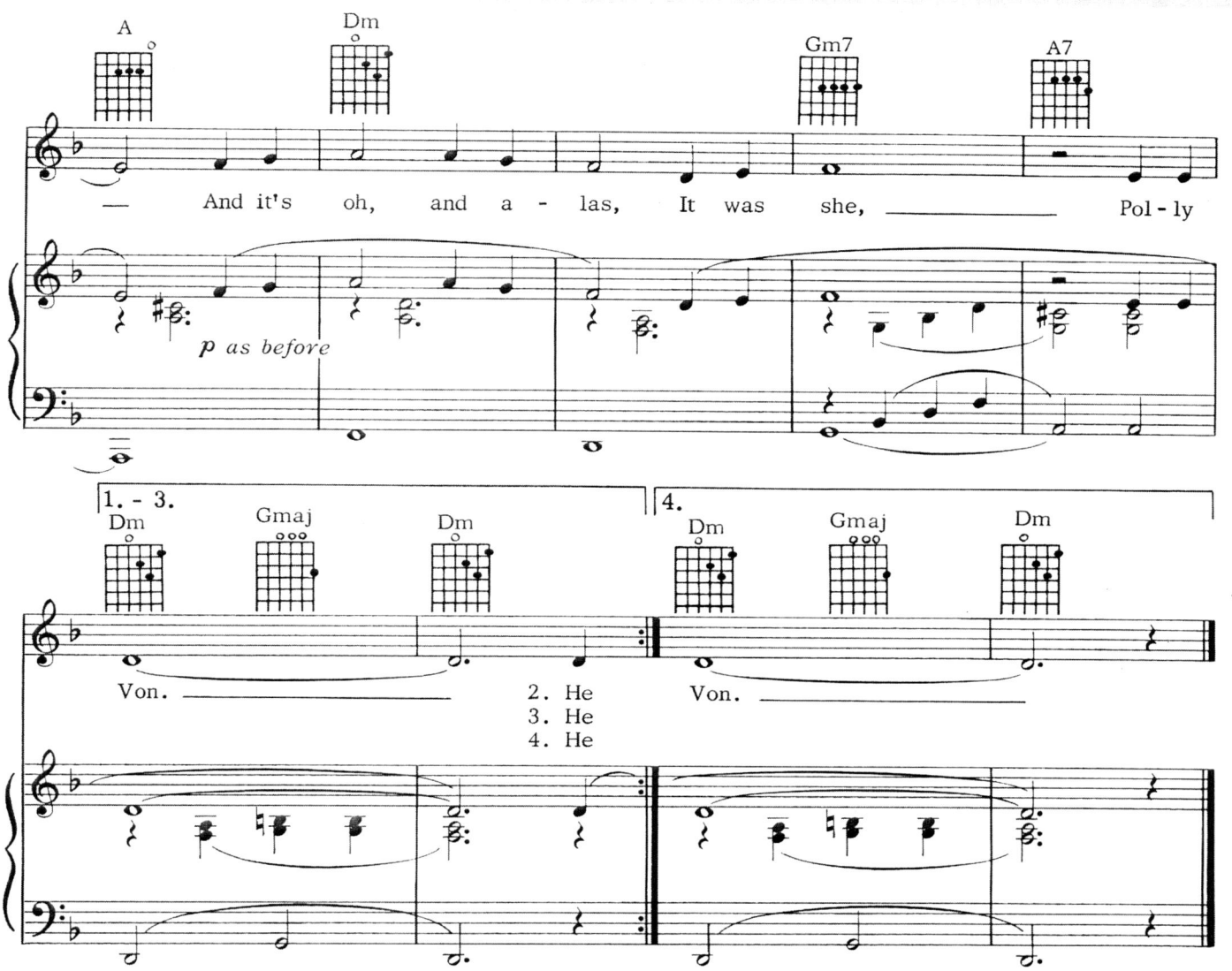

2. He ran up beside her,
   And found it was she,
   He turned away his head
   For he could not bear to see,
   He lifted her up
   And found she was dead,
   A fountain of tears
   For his true love he shed.

   REFRAIN

3. He bore her away
   To his home by the sea
   And "Father, oh Father
   I've murdered poor Polly.
   I've killed my fair love
   In the flower of her life,
   I'd always intended
   That she be my wife."

   REFRAIN

4. He roamed near the place
   Where his true love was slain,
   He wept bitter tears
   But his cries were all in vain,
   As he looked on the lake
   A swan glided by
   And the sun slowly sank
   In the grey of the sky.

   REFRAIN

Tell It on the Mountain

ADAPTED AND ARRANGED BY PETER YARROW, PAUL STOOKEY, MARY TRAVERS AND MILTON OKUN

© 1963, 1964 PEPAMAR MUSIC CORP.
Copyrights Renewed
All Rights Reserved

All My Trials

ADAPTED AND ARRANGED BY PETER YARROW, PAUL STOOKEY AND MILTON OKUN

Very Last Day

WORDS AND MUSIC BY PAUL STOOKEY AND PETER YARROW

© 1963, 1964 PEPAMAR MUSIC CORP.
Copyrights Renewed
All Rights Reserved

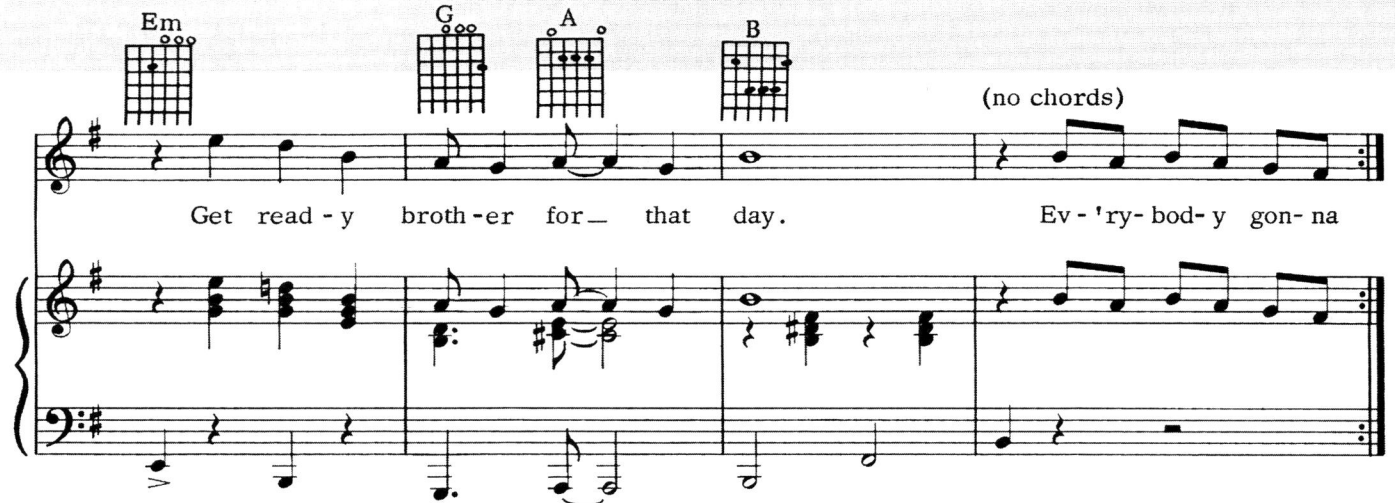

2. Well one day soon all men will stand,
   His word will be heeded in all the land,
   Men shall know and men shall seek,
   We all are brothers and we all are free
   Mankind was made of clay,
   Each of us in the very same way,
   Get ready, brother, for that day.

   REFRAIN

3. Oh well the law is given and the law is known,
   A tale is told and the seed is sown,
   From dust we came and to dust will go,
   You know the Lord once told us so.
   Each brother takes His hand,
   Heed the meaning of the Lord's command
   Get ready, brother, for that day.

   REFRAIN

Quit Your Low Down Ways

BY BOB DYLAN

Copyright © 1963 WARNER BROS. Inc.
Copyright Renewed 1991 by SPECIAL RIDER MUSIC
International Copyright Secured   All Rights Reserved
Used by Permission

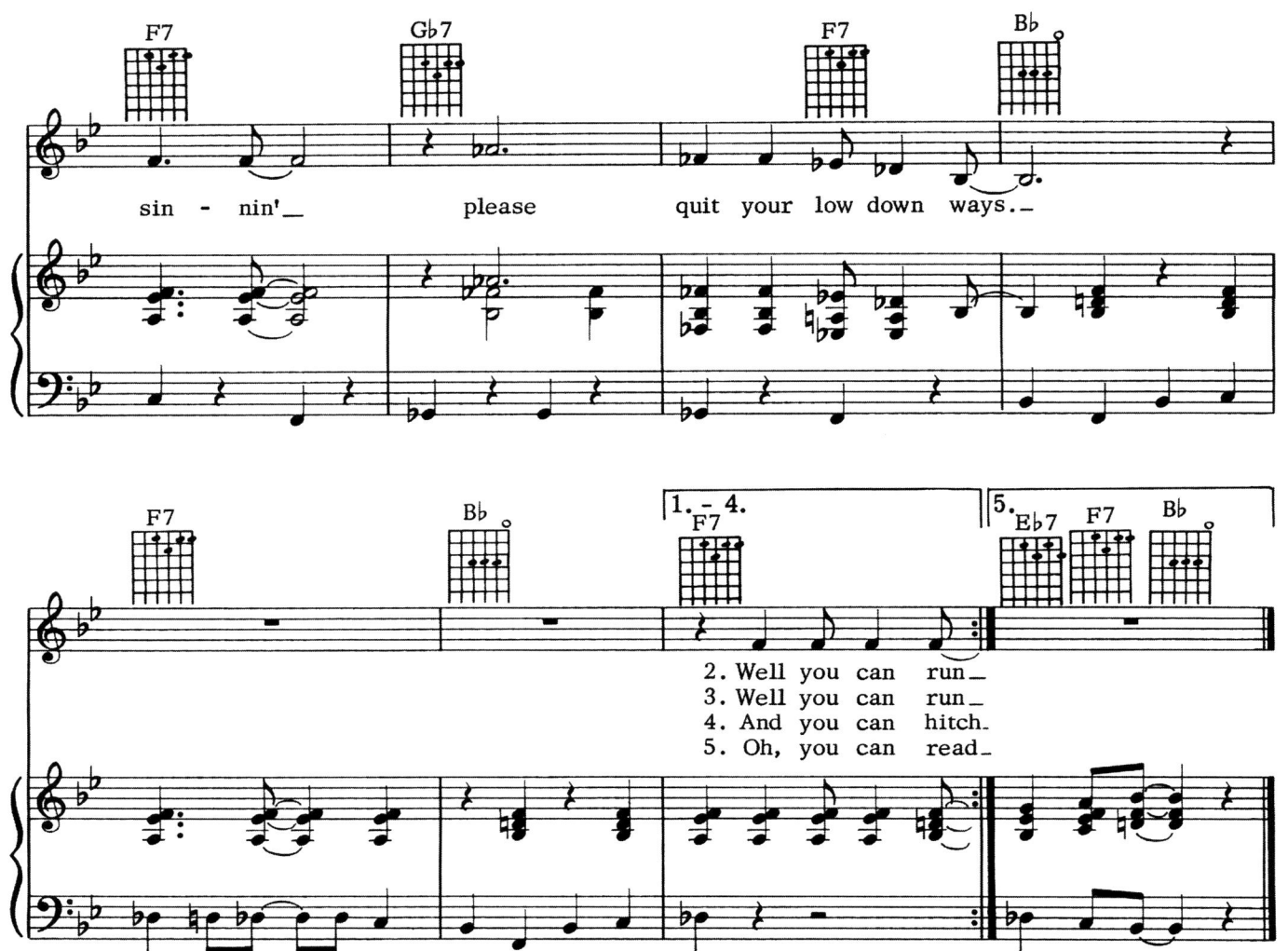

2. Well, you can run down to the White House,
   You can gaze at the Capitol Dome, pretty mama,
   You can pound on the President's gate
   But you oughta know by now it's gonna be too late.

   REFRAIN

3. Well, you can run down to the desert,
   Throw yourself on the burning sand,
   You can raise up your right hand, pretty mama,
   But you better understand you done lost your one
                    good man.

   REFRAIN

4. And you can hitch hike on the highway,
   You can stand all alone by the side of the road,
   You can try to flag a ride back home, pretty mama,
   But you can't ride in my car no more.

   REFRAIN

5. Oh, you can read out your Bible,
   You can fall down on your knees, pretty mama,
   And pray to the Lord
   But it ain't gonna do no good.

   REFRAIN

Oh, Rock My Soul

ADAPTED AND ARRANGED BY PETER YARROW

© 1964 PEPAMAR MUSIC CORP. (Renewed)
All Rights Reserved

2. Come writers and critics
   Who prophecies with your pen
   And keep your eyes wide
   The chance won't come again.
   And don't speak too soon
   For the wheel's still in spin
   And there's no tellin' who
   That it's namin'
   For the loser now
   Will be later to win
   For the times they are a-changin'.

3. Come senators, congressmen
   Please heed the call
   Don't stand in the doorway
   Don't block up the hall.
   For he that gets hurt
   Will be he who has stalled
   There's a battle
   Outside and it's ragin'
   It'll soon shake your windows
   And rattle your walls
   For the times they are a-changin'.

4. Come mothers and fathers,
   Throughout the land
   And don't criticize
   What you can't understand.
   Your sons and your daughters
   Are beyond your command
   Your old road is
   Rapidly agin'
   Please get out of the new one
   If you can't lend your hand
   For the times they are a-changin'.

5. The line it is drawn
   The curse it is cast
   The slow one now will
   Later be fast.
   As the present now
   Will later be past
   The order is rapidly fadin'
   And the first one now
   Will later be last
   For the times they are a-changin'.

Blue

ADAPTED AND ARRANGED BY PETER YARROW, PAUL STOOKEY AND MARY TRAVERS

Dialogue: We'd like to sing a children's song for you now. It's unique. It's the only children's song that we have ever encountered that contains all three of the basic elements of every single children's song. The first element is simplicity--so that the child can understand the song. The second element is pathos--to prepare the child for later traumatic experiences and the third element is repetition--to give the child a false sense of security.

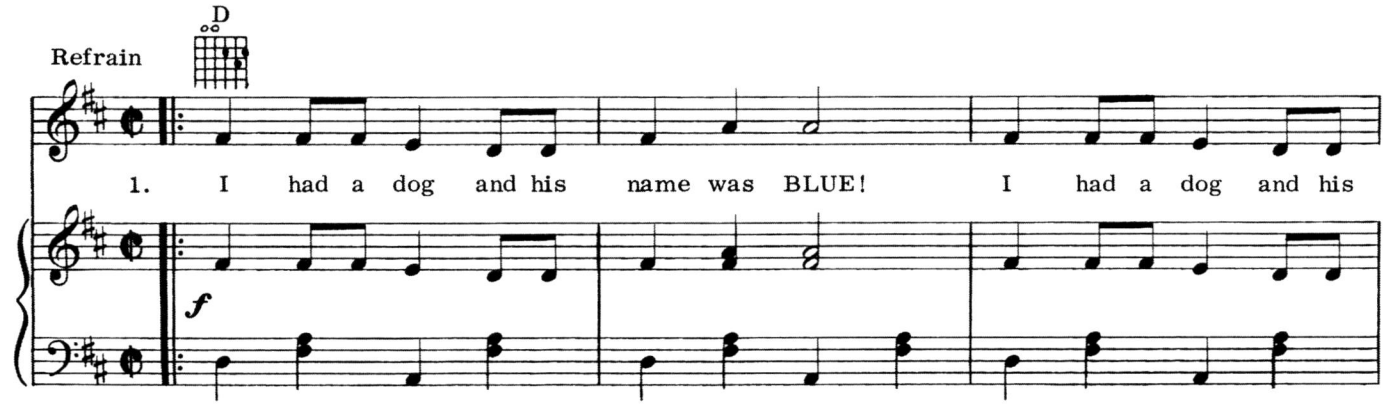

© 1964 PEPAMAR MUSIC CORP. (Renewed)
All Rights Reserved

Refrain 2. Old Blue come when I blow my horn
Old Blue come when I blow my horn
Blue come a runnin' through the yellow corn
Blue come a runnin' when I blow my horn
Singin' here Blue you're a good dog you.

Dialogue: What if this song were to be changed? Modified by an unscrupulous modifier of folk songs whose business it is to make this type of song palatable for the teenage delinquent "mother-my-dog" instinct. Then it would be a rock 'n roll song. Oh nasty unscrupulous modifier! Now it would sound something like this:

One Kind Favor

ADAPTED AND ARRANGED BY PETER YARROW, PAUL STOOKEY AND MARY TRAVERS

* Guitar chords as played by Peter, Paul & Mary.

© 1964 PEPAMAR MUSCI CORP. (Renewed)
All Rights Reserved

2. There's two white horses in a line
There's two white horses in a line
There's two white horses in a line
Carryin' me to my buryin' ground.

4. Have you ever heard a coffin sound
Have you ever heard a coffin sound
Have you ever heard a coffin sound
Bein' lowered in the ground?

3. There's three black coaches in the rain
There's three black coaches in the rain
There's three black coaches in the rain
Empty now from their heavy load.

5. There's one kind of favor I'll ask of you
There's one kind of favor I'll ask of you
There's one kind of favor I'll ask of you
See that my grave is kept clean.

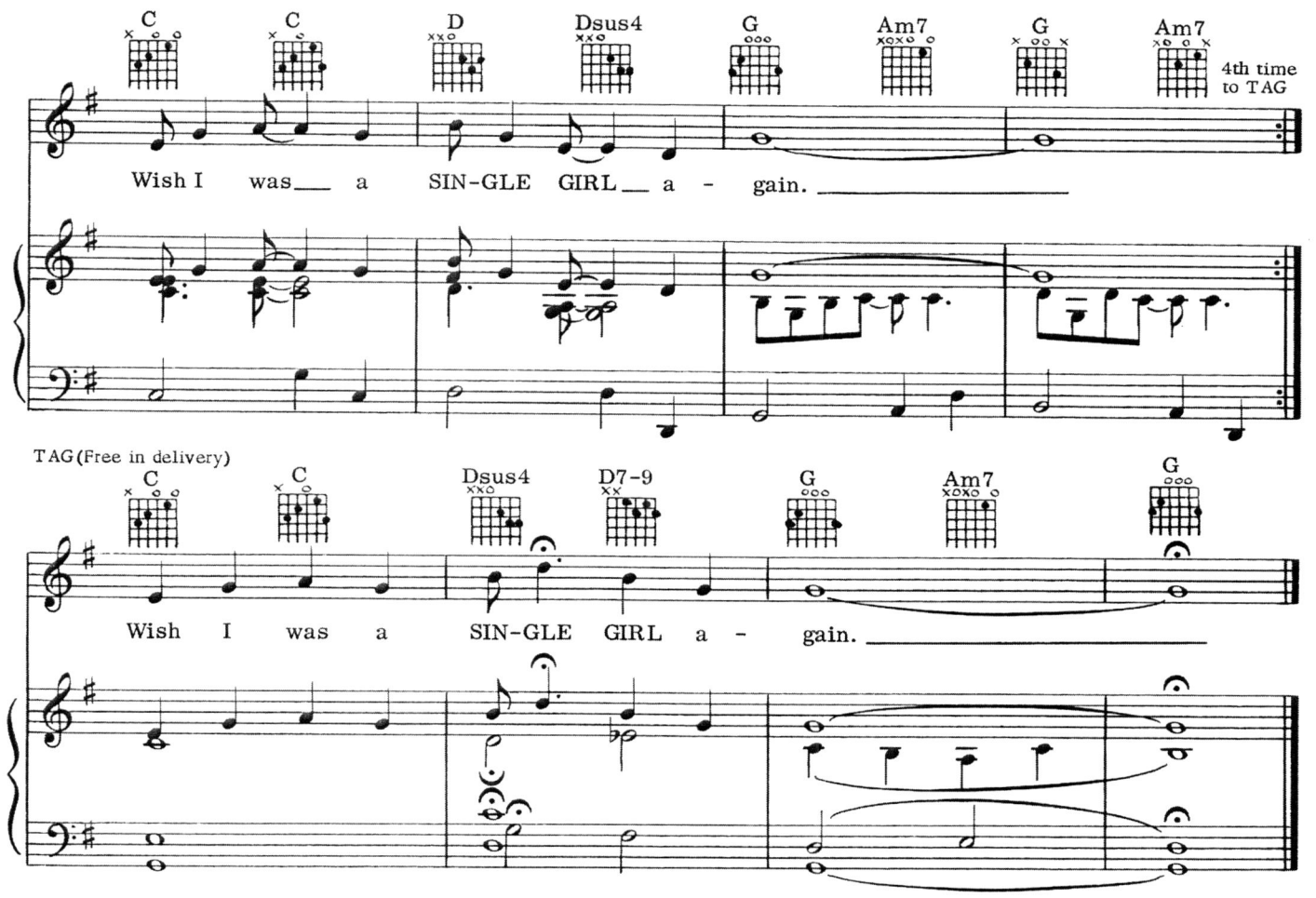

2. When I was a single girl,
   Had shoes of the very best kind,
   Now I am a married girl,
   Go barefoot all the time.
   Wish I was a single girl again,
   Wish I was a single girl again.

3. When I was a single girl,
   Used to go to the store and buy,
   Now I am a married girl,
   Just rock that cradle and cry.
   Wish I was a single girl again,
   Wish I was a single girl again.

4. When a fella comes a-courtin' you,
   And sits you on his knee,
   Keep your eye upon the sparrow,
   That flits from tree to tree.
   And you'll never wish you were a single girl like me,
   You'll never wish you were a single girl like me.

Three Ravens

ADAPTED AND ARRANGED BY PETER YARROW, PAUL STOOKEY, MILTON OKUN & MARY TRAVERS

*Guitar chords as played by Peter, Paul & Mary.

© 1964 PEPAMAR MUSIC CORP. (Renewed)
All Rights Reserved

2. Down in yonder green field,
   Down-a-down, Hey! Down-a-down,
   There lies a knight slain under his shield, with a down.

   Down there comes a fallow doe,
   As great with young as she might go
   With a down derry derry derry, down-down.

3. She lifted up his bloody head,
   Down-a-down, Hey! Down-a-down,
   And kissed his wounds that were so red, with a down.

   She got him up across her back
   And carried him to the earthen lack*
   With a down derry derry derry, down-down.

4. She buried him before his prime,
   Down-a-down, Hey! Down-a-down,
   She was dead, herself, ere evening time, with a down.

   God send every gentleman
   Fine hawks, fine hounds and such a loved one
   With a down derry derry derry, down, Hmm.

* lack means lake (archaic pronunciation)

There Is a Ship

ADAPTED AND ARRANGED BY PETER YARROW, PAUL STOOKEY, MARY TRAVERS AND MILTON OKUN

© 1964 PEPAMAR MUSIC CORP. (Renewed)
All Rights Reserved

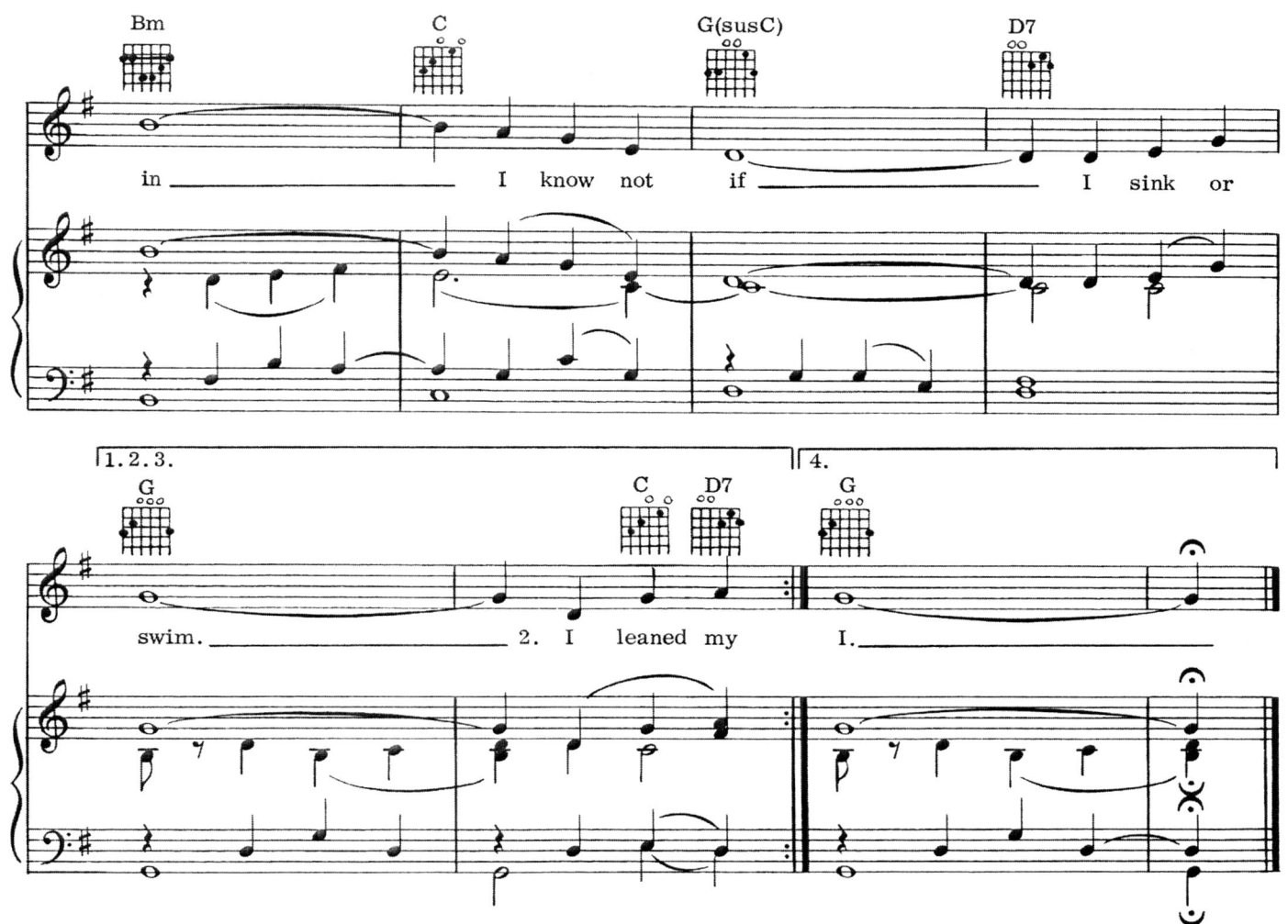

2. I leaned my back against an oak,
   Thinking it was a trusty tree,
   But first it bent and then it broke,
   Just as my love proved false to me.

3. Oh, love is gentle, and love is kind,
   The sweetest flow'r when first it's new;
   But love grows old and waxes cold,
   And fades away like the mornin' dew.

4. The water is wide, I can not get o'er,
   Neither have I the wings to fly,
   Give me a boat that can carry two,
   And both shall row my love and I.

Jesus Met the Woman

ADAPTED AND ARRANGED BY PETER YARROW, MARY TRAVERS AND MILTON OKUN

© 1964 PEPAMAR MUSIC CORP. (Renewed)
All Rights Reserved

Verse 2. She said: "Jesus, Jesus, I ain't got no husband."
She said: "Jesus, Jesus, I ain't got no husband."
She said: "Jesus, Jesus, ain't got no husband
And You don't know ev'rything I've ever done."

Verse 3. He said: "Woman, woman, you've got five husbands."
He said: "Woman, woman, you've got five husbands."
He said: "Woman, woman, you've got five husbands
And the one you have now, he's not your own."

Verse 4. She said: "This man, this man, He must be a prophet."
She said: "This man, this man, He must be a prophet,
This man, this man must be a prophet,
He done told me ev'rything I've ever done."

Refrain.

Gilgarra Mountain

ADAPTED AND ARRANGED BY PETER YARROW

© 1965 PEPAMAR MUSIC CORP. (Renewed)
All Rights Reserved

2. He counted out his money
   And it made a pretty penny
   I put it in my pocket
   To take home to darlin' Jenny.

   She sighed and swore she loved me
   And never would deceive me
   But the devil take the women
   For they always lie so easy.
   Refrain

3. I went into me chamber
   All for to take a slumber
   To dream of gold and girls
   And of course it was no wonder

   Me Jenny took me charges
   And she filled them up with water
   Called on Colonel Farrell
   To get ready for the slaughter.
   Refrain

4. Next morning early
   Before I rose for travel
   A-came a band of footmen
   And likewise Colonel Farrell

   I goes to draw my pistol
   For she'd stole away my rapier
   But a prisoner I was taken
   I couldn't shoot the water.
   Refrain

5. They put me into jail
   With a judge all a-writin'
   Robbin' Colonel Farrell
   On Gilgarra Mountain

   But they didn't take me fists
   And I knocked the jailer down
   And bid a farewell
   To this tight fisted town.
   Refrain

6. I'd like to find me brother
   The one that's in the army
   I don't know where he's stationed
   In Cork or in Killarney

   Together we'd go roamin'
   O'er the mountains of Kilkenny
   And I swear he'd treat me fairer
   Than me darlin' sportin' Jenny.
   Refrain

7. There's some takes delight
   In the carriages and rollin'
   Some takes delight
   In the hurley or the bollin'

   But I takes delight
   In the juice of the barley
   Courtin' pretty maids
   In the mornin', oh so early.
   Refrain

Jimmy Whalen

ADAPTED AND ARRANGED BY PETER YARROW, PAUL STOOKEY, MARY TRAVERS AND MILTON OKUN

© 1965 PEPAMAR MUSIC CORP. (Renewed)
All Rights Reserved

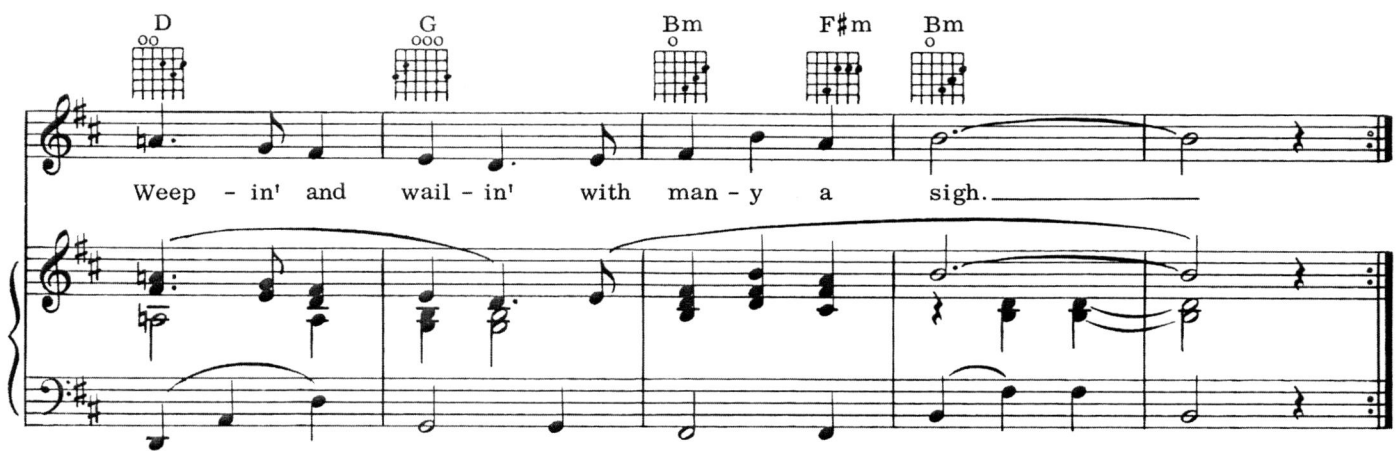

Weep - in' and wail - in' with man - y a sigh.

2. Weepin' for one who is now lyin' lonely
   Mournin' for one who no mortal can save
   As the foaming dark waters flowed sadly about him
   Onward they speed over young Jimmy's grave.

3. Oh Jimmy why can't you but tarry here with me
   Not leave me alone distracted in pain
   But since death is the dagger that cut us asunder
   Wide is the gulf, love, between you and I.

The Cuckoo

WORDS AND MUSIC BY DWAIN STORY, ERIK JACOBSEN, PETER YARROW, PAUL STOOKEY, MARY TRAVERS & MILTON OKUN

© 1963, 1965 PEPAMAR MUSIC CORP. (Renewed)
All Rights Reserved

2. I've gambled in England
   And I've gambled in Spain,
   I've gambled with five aces,
   Now I've gambled my last game.

4. Jack O' Diamonds, Jack O' Diamonds,
   I know you of old,
   You robbed my poor pockets
   Of silver and of gold.

3. Oh it's gamblin' that's brought me prison
   And it's gamblin' that's brought me pain,
   I'll never see the Cuckoo
   Or hear her song again.

5. Oh the Cuckoo, she's a pretty bird,
   She sings as she flies,
   She never gets lonesome
   Till the first day of July.

Monday Morning

ADAPTED AND ARRANGED BY PETER YARROW, PAUL STOOKEY, MARY TRAVERS AND MILTON OKUN

© 1965 PEPAMAR MUSIC CORP. (Renewed)
All Rights Reserved

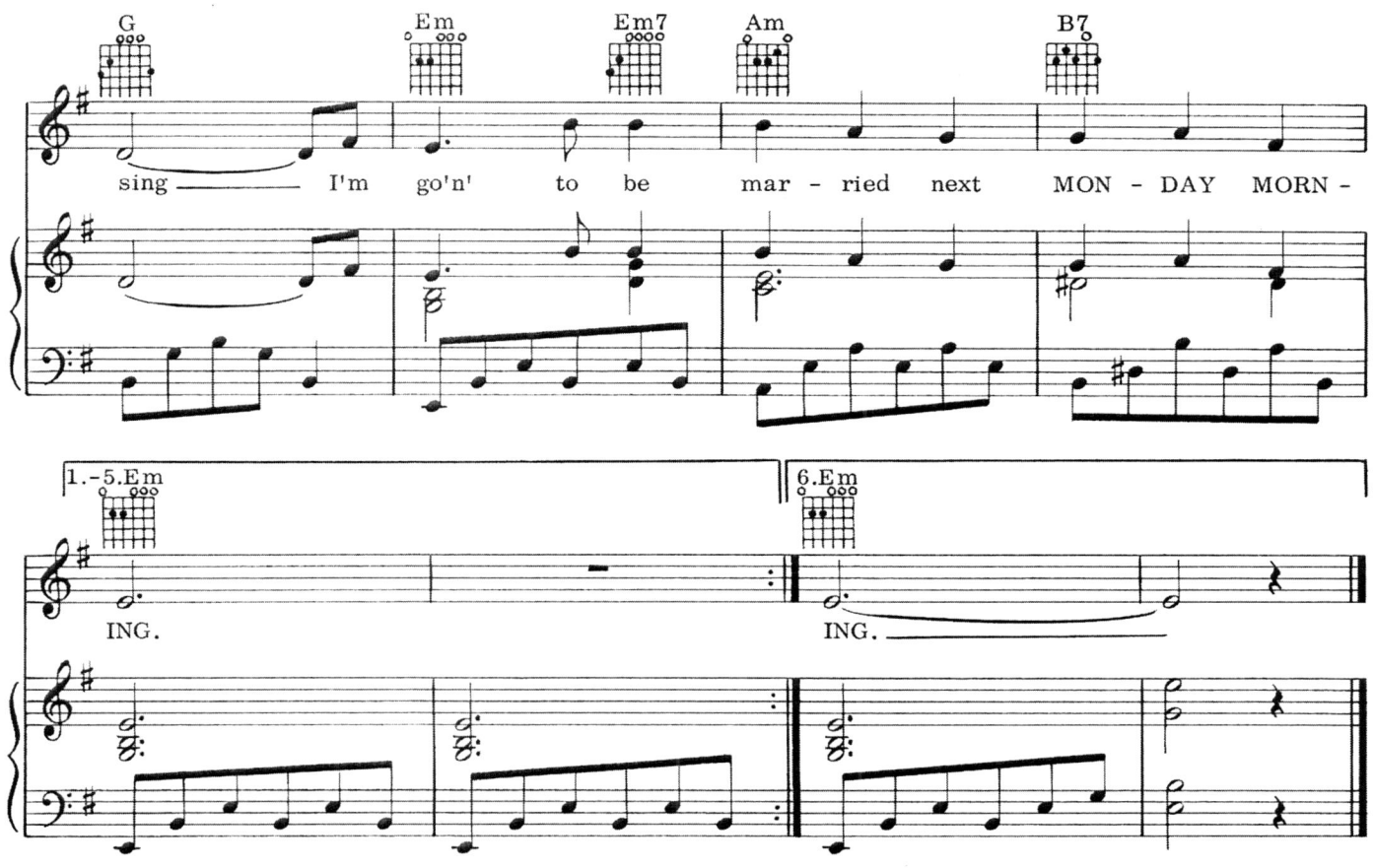

2. How old are you my fair young maid
   Here in this valley, this valley so green?
   How old are you my fair young maid?
   I'm going to be sixteen next Monday morning.

3. Well sixteen years old that's too young for to marry
   So take my advice five years longer to tarry,
   For marriage brings troubles and sorrows begin,
   So put off your wedding for Monday morning.

4. You talk like a mad man, a man with no skill;
   Five years I've been waiting against my own will,
   But now I'm determined to have my own way
   And I'm going to be married next Monday morning.

5. Next Monday morning the bells they will ring,
   My true love will buy me a gay gold ring;
   Also he'll buy me a new pretty gown
   To wear at my wedding next Monday morning.

6. Next Monday night when I go to my bed
   And I turn 'round to the man that I've wed,
   Around his middle my two arms I will fling
   And I wish to my soul it was Monday morning.

Motherless Child

ADAPTED AND ARRANGED BY MARY TRAVERS AND MILTON OKUN

© 1965 PEPAMAR MUSIC CORP. (Renewed)
All Rights Reserved

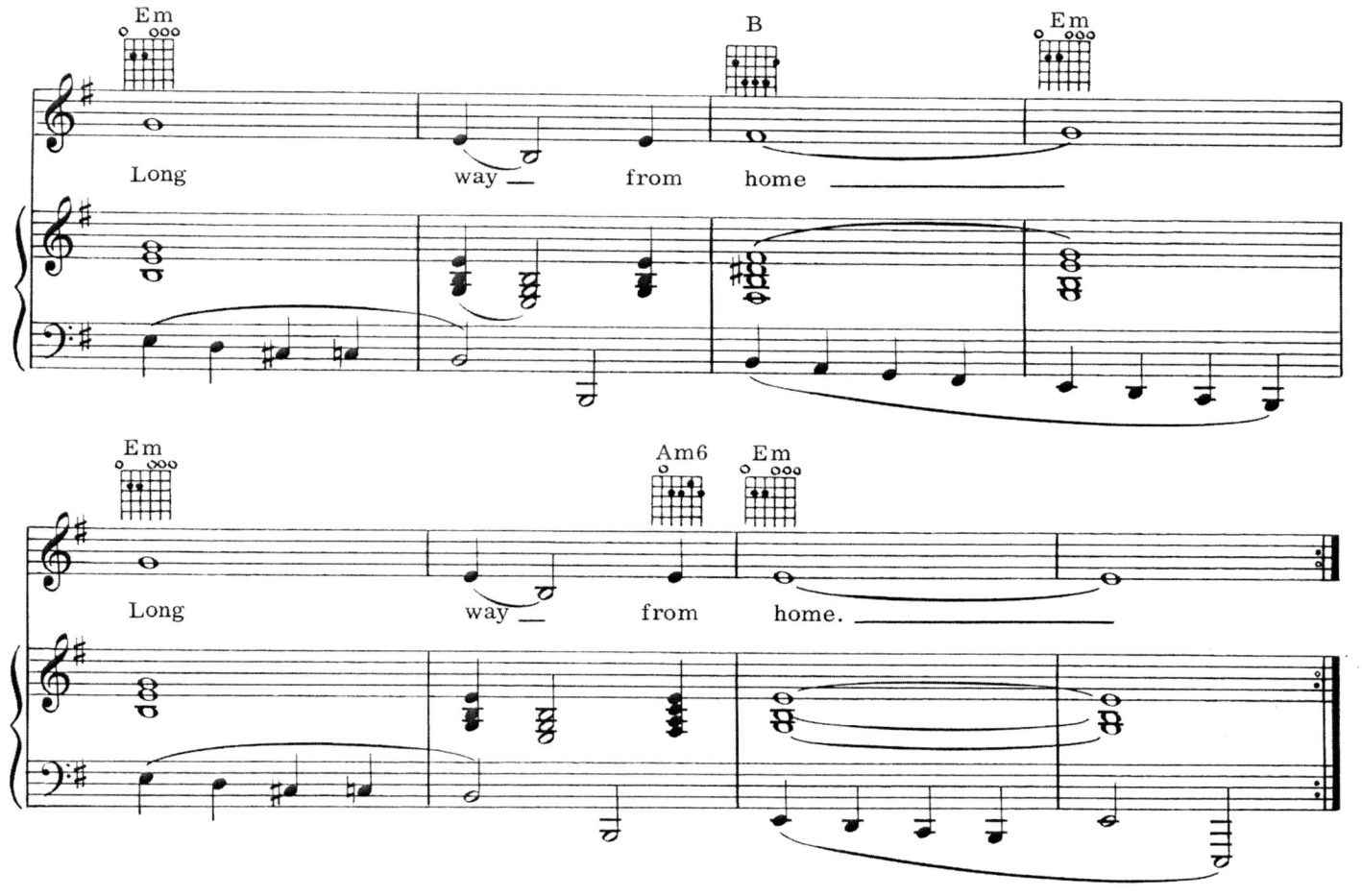

2. Sometimes I feel like I'm almost gone
   Sometimes I feel like I'm almost gone
   Sometimes I feel like I'm almost gone
   Long way from home, long way from home.

3. Sometimes I feel like a mournin' dove
   Sometimes I feel like a mournin' dove
   Sometimes I feel like a mournin' dove
   Long way from home, long way from home.

4. Sometimes I feel like an eagle in the air
   Sometimes I feel like an eagle in the air
   Sometimes I feel like an eagle in the air
   Long way from home, long way from home.

5. Sometimes I feel like a motherless child
   Sometimes I feel like a motherless child
   Sometimes I feel like a motherless child
   Long way from home, long way from home.

Come and Go With Me

ADAPTED AND ARRANGED BY PETER YARROW, PAUL STOOKEY, MARY TRAVERS AND MILTON OKUN

© 1965 PEPAMAR MUSIC CORP. (Renewed)
All Rights Reserved

Verse 2.   There ain't no kneelin' in that land
           There ain't no kneelin' in that land
           There ain't no kneelin' in that land
           Where I'm bound.
           There ain't no kneelin' in that land
           There ain't no kneelin' in that land
           Kneelin' in that land
           Where I'm bound.

Verse 3.   There'll be singin' in that land
           Voices ringin' in that land
           There'll be freedom in that land
           Where I'm bound.
           There'll be singin' in that land
           There'll be singin' in that land
           Freedom in that land
           Where I'm bound.

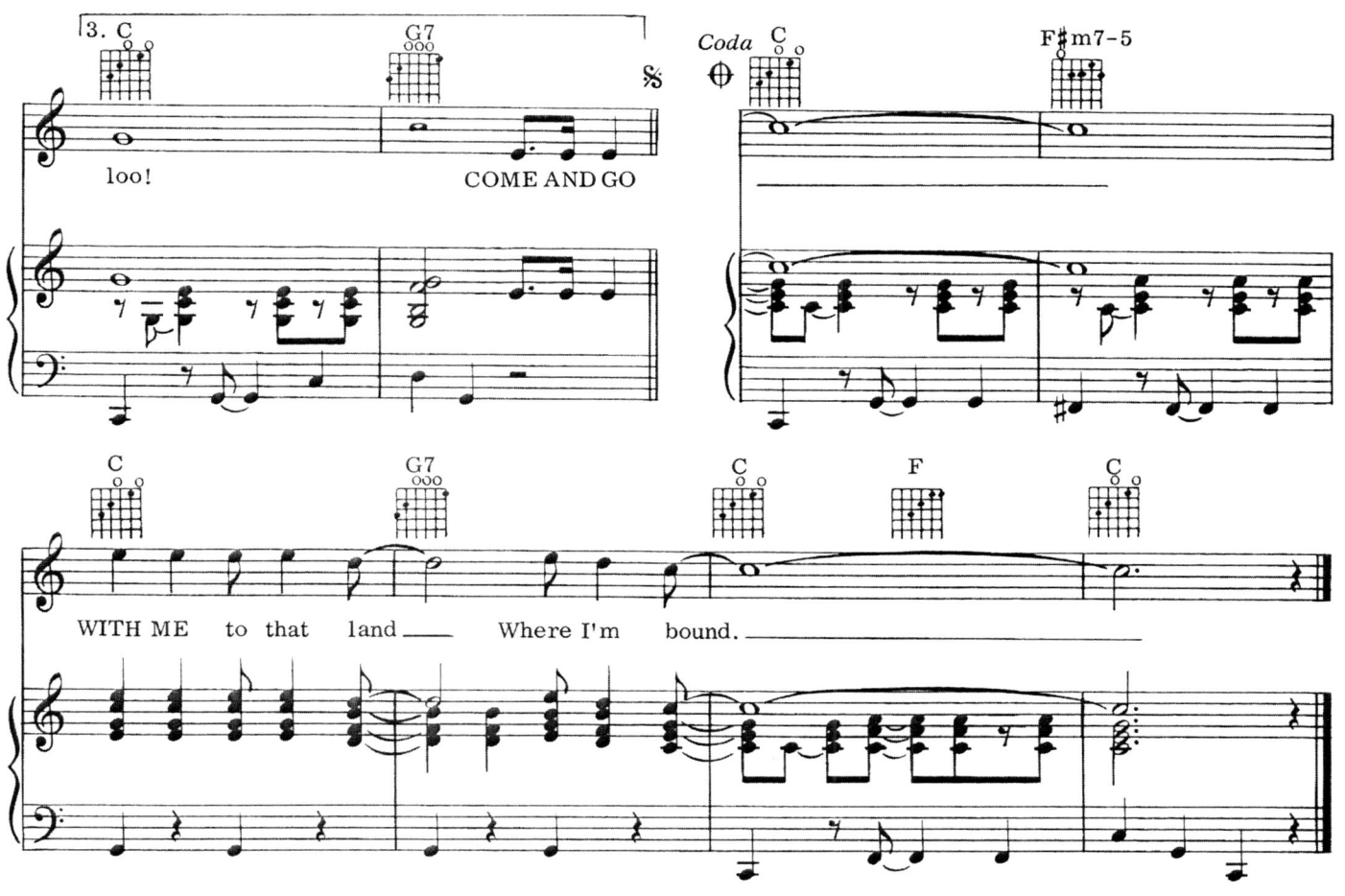

2nd Refrain: Don't you wanna hear the children singin'
On that great day in the mornin'
Don't you wanna hear the children singin'
On that great day in the mornin'
Don't you wanna hear all the children singin'
Jingle bells are ringin'
Don't you wanna hear all the children singin'
Halleloo!

3rd Refrain: Don't you wanna stand in line together
On that great day in the mornin'
Don't you wanna stand in line together
On that great day in the mornin'
Don't you wanna stand in line together
Shake hands with one another
Don't you wanna stand in line together
Halleloo!

For Lovin' Me

BY GORDON LIGHTFOOT

© 1964, 1965 MOOSE MUSIC LTD.
Copyrights Renewed
All Rights Reserved

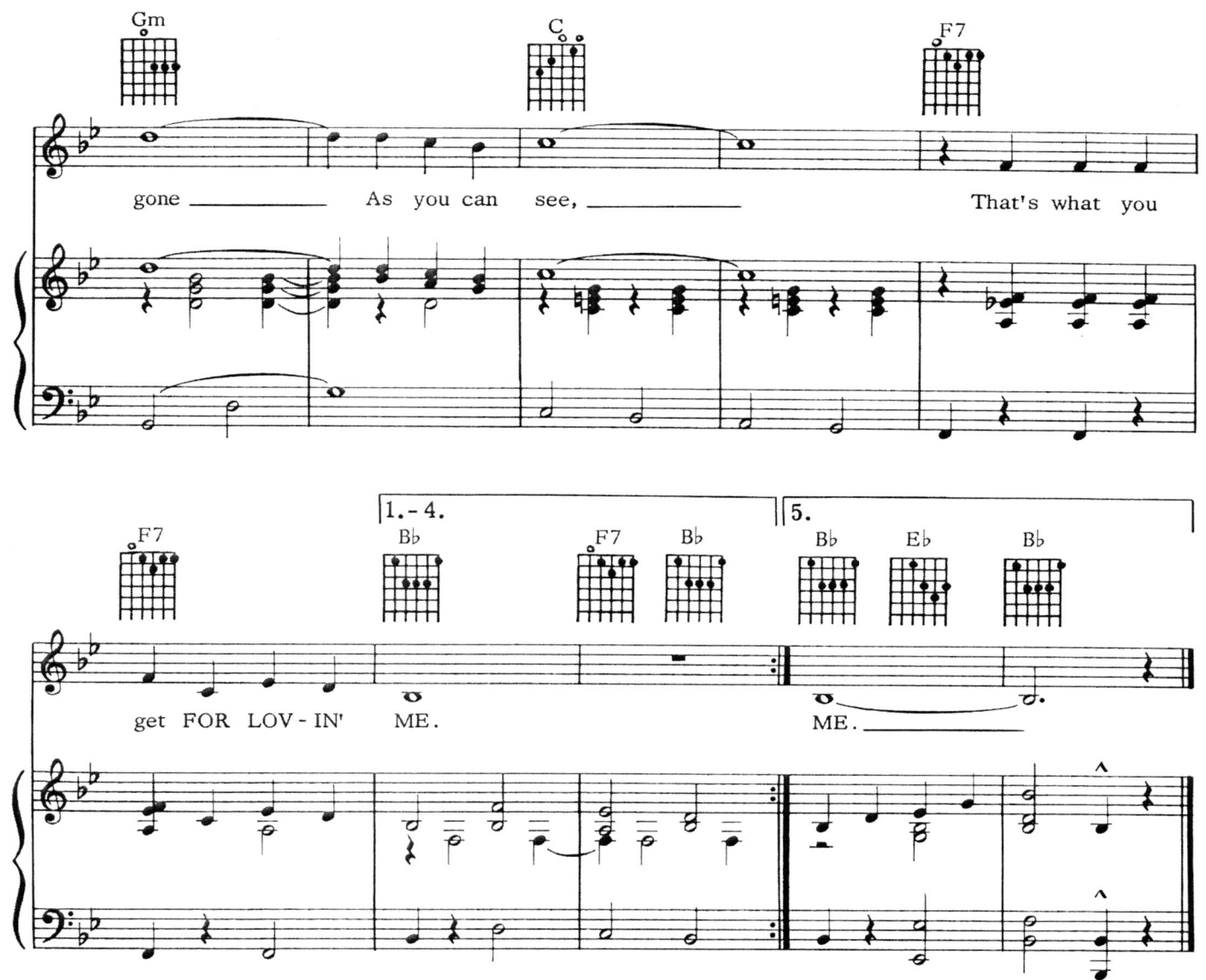

2. I ain't the kind to hang around
   With any new love that I found
   'Cause movin' is my stock in trade
   I'm movin' on,
   I won't think of you when I'm gone.

3. So don't you shed a tear for me,
   I ain't the love you thought I'd be,
   I got a hundred more like you,
   So don't be blue,
   I'll have a thousand 'fore I'm through.

4. Now, there you go you're cryin' again,
   Now, there you go you're cryin' again,
   But then, some day, when your poor heart
   Is on the mend,
   Well, I just might pass this way again.

5. That's what you get for lovin' me,
   That's what you get for lovin' me,
   Well, ev'rything you had is gone
   As you can see,
   That's what you get for lovin' me.

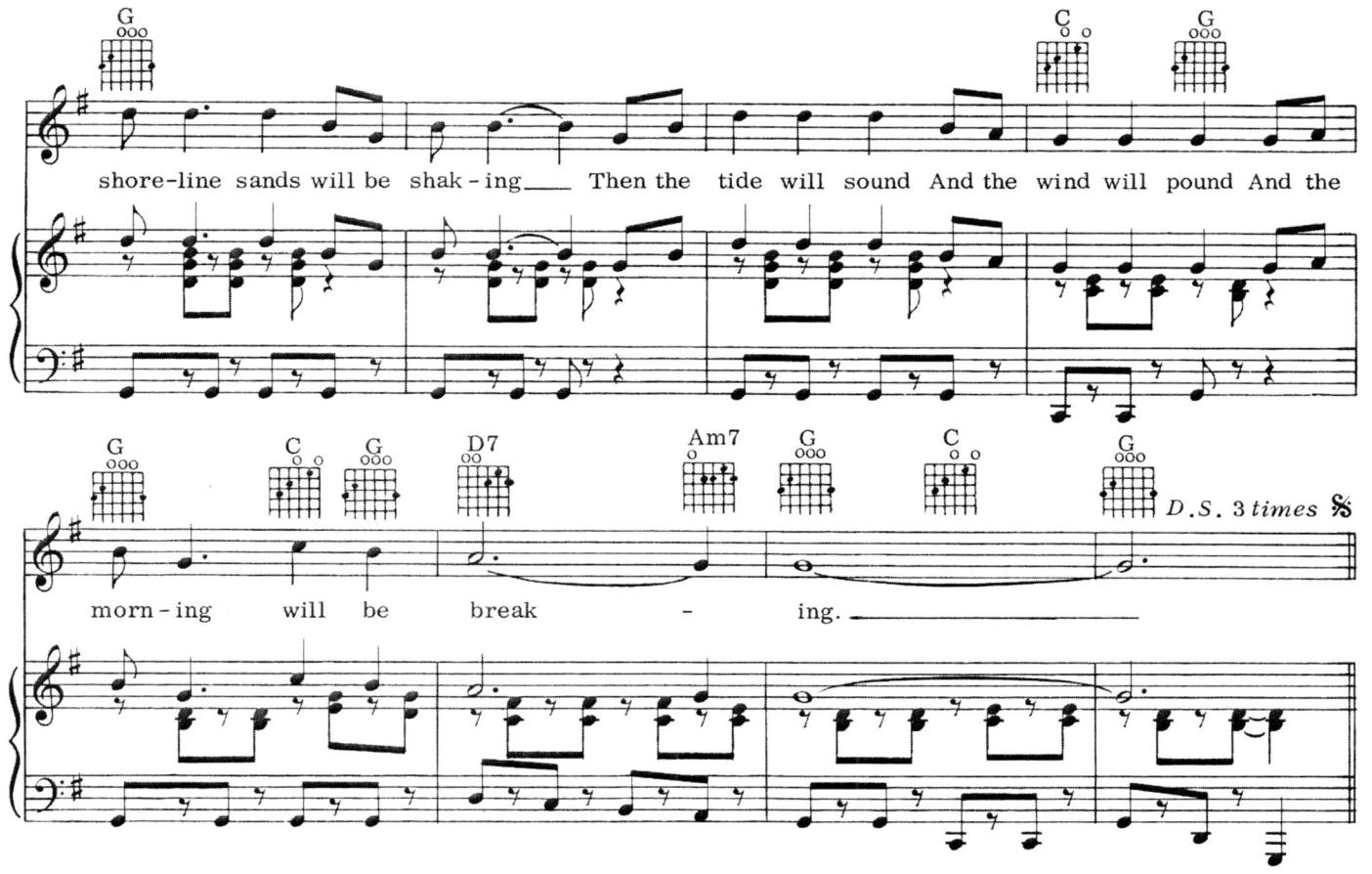

2. Oh the fishes will laugh
   As they swim out of the path
   And the seagulls they'll be smiling
   And the rocks on the sand
   Will proudly stand
   The hour that the ship comes in.

   And the words they use
   For to get the ship confused
   Will not be understood as they're spoken
   For the chains of the sea
   Will have busted in the night
   And will be buried at the bottom of the ocean.

3. A song will lift
   As the mainsail shifts
   And the boat drifts on to the shore line
   And the sun will respect
   Every face on the deck
   The hour when the ship comes in.

   Then the sands will roll
   Out a carpet of gold
   For your weary toes to be a touchin'
   And the ship's wise men
   Will remind you once again
   That the whole wide world is watchin'.

4. Oh the foes will rise
   With the sleep still in their eyes
   And they'll jerk from their beds and think they're dreamin'
   But they'll pinch themselves and squeal
   And know that it's for real
   The hour when the ship comes in.

   Then they'll raise their hands
   Sayin' we'll meet all your demands
   But we'll shout from the bow your days are numbered
   And like Pharoah's triumph
   They'll be drownded in the tide
   And like Goliath they'll be conquered.

PETER, PAUL & MARY ALBUMS FOR WARNER BROS. RECORDS

PETER, PAUL & MARY
W. B. 1449

Early in the Morning • 500 miles • Sorrow • This Train • Bamboo • It's Raining • If I Had My Way • Cruel War • Lemon Tree • If I Had a Hammer • Autumn to May • Where Have All the Flowers Gone

PETER, PAUL & MARY MOVING
W. B. 1473

Settle Down • Gone the Rainbow • Flora • Pretty Mary • Puff • This Land Is Your Land • Man Come into Egypt • Old Coat • Tiny Sparrow • Big Boat • Morning Train • A 'Soalin'

PETER, PAUL & MARY IN THE WIND
W. B. 1507

Very Last Day • Hush-A-Bye • Long Chain On • Rocky Road • Tell It on the Mountain • Polly Von • Stewball • All My Trials • Don't Think Twice, It's All Right • Freight Train • Quit Your Low Down Ways • Blowin' in the Wind

PETER, PAUL & MARY IN CONCERT
W. B. 1555

The Times They Are A'Changin' • A'Soalin' • 500 Miles • Blue • 3 Ravens • One Kind Favor • Blowin' in the Wind • Car-Car • Puff • Jesus Met the Woman • Le Deserteur • Oh, Rock My Soul • Paultalk • Single Girl • There Is a Ship • It's Raining • If I Had My Way • If I Had a Hammer

PETER, PAUL & MARY A SONG WILL RISE
W. B. 1589

When the Ship Comes In • For Lovin' Me • Monday Morning • Jimmy Whalen • Come and Go with Me • Motherless Child • The Cuckoo • Gilgarry Mountain • Ballad of Spring Hill • Wasn't That a Time • San Francisco Bay Blues • Talkin' Candy Bar Blues

INDEX OF FIRST LINES

All alone as I walked	122
All my trials, Lord	90
As I was a-goin' over Gilgarra Mountain	119
Come all ye fair and tender ladies	65
Come and go with me to that land	130
Come gather 'round people wherever you roam	102
Early one morning	126
Ev'rybody gonna pray	94
Go tell it on the mountain	82
Hey-ho, nobody home	50
How many roads must a man walk down	44
Hush-a-bye, Don't you cry	71
I am a man of constant sorrow	30
I had a dog and his name was Blue	104
I looked to the east, I looked to the west	58
I'm goin' home on the morning train	54
I shall tell of a hunter	79
It ain't no use to sit and wonder why, Babe	46
It's raining, it's pouring	32
I went up the levee to pack some sacks	86
Jesus met the woman at the well	116

My horses ain't hungry	62
Oh, once I had a little dog	20
Oh the cuckoo, She's a pretty bird	124
Oh the time will come up	136
Oh, you can read out your Bible	96
Puff, the magic dragon lived by the sea	41
Red light, green light, 'round the town	74
Rock my soul in the bosom of Abraham	99
Shule, shule, shule-a-roo	17
Sometimes I feel like a motherless child	128
That's what you get for lovin' me	134
The cruel war is raging	28
There is a ship	114
There's one kind favor I'll ask for you	108
There were three ravens, sat on a tree	112
This train don't carry on gam-b-lers	14
Well early in the mornin'	12
When first I came to Louisville	68
When I was a single girl	110
You read about Samson	23
You take a stick of bamboo	38

CHORD DIAGRAMS FOR UKULELE AND BARITONE UKULELE USED IN THIS FOLIO

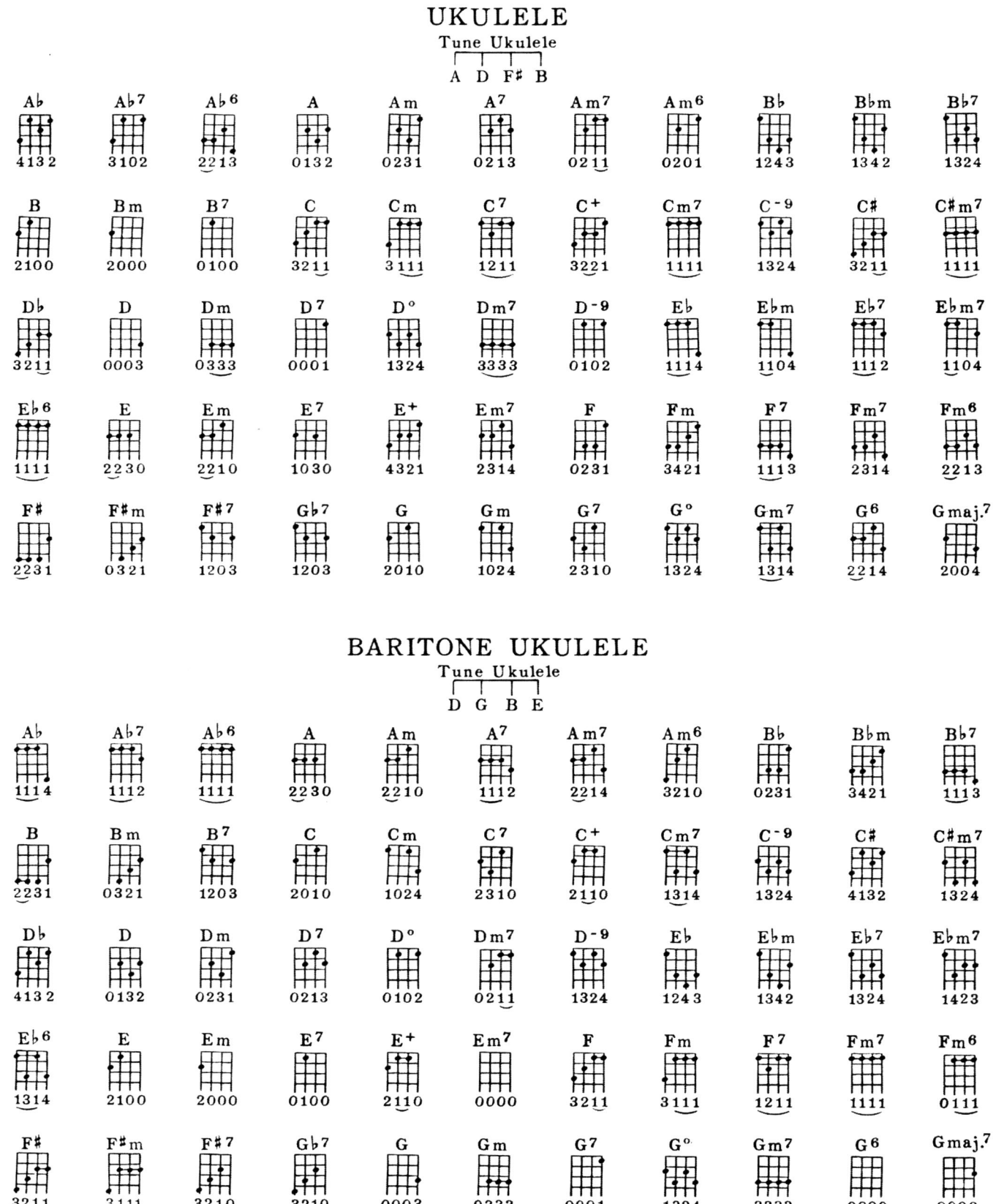

CHORD DIAGRAMS FOR
TENOR BANJO AND FIVE STRING BANJO USED IN THIS FOLIO

TENOR BANJO

FIVE STRING BANJO
(C TUNING)